Collins

Caribbean Social Studies 1

Jain Cook

HarperCollins *Publishers* Ltd
The News Building
1 London Bridge Street
London SE1 9GF

First edition 2017

10 9 8 7 6 5 4 3 2 1

© HarperCollins *Publishers* Limited 2017

ISBN 978-0-00-825649-4

Collins® is a registered trademark of HarperCollins *Publishers* Limited

www.collins.co.uk/caribbeanschools

A catalogue record for this book is available from the British Library.

Printed by Grafica Veneta SpA in Italy

All rights reserved. No part of this book may be reproduced, stored in a retrieval system, or transmitted in any form or by any means, electronic, mechanical, photocopying, recording or otherwise, without the prior permission in writing of the Publisher. This book is sold subject to the conditions that it shall not, by way of trade or otherwise, be lent, re-sold, hired out or otherwise circulated without the Publisher's prior consent in any form of binding or cover other than that in which it is published and without a similar condition including this condition being imposed on the subsequent purchaser.

If any copyright holders have been omitted, please contact the Publisher who will make the necessary arrangements at the first opportunity.

Author: Jain Cook
Series Editor: Cherril Barrett-Field
Typesetting and illustration: QBS Learning
Publisher: Elaine Higgleton
Commissioning Editor: Bruce Nicholson
In-house Senior Editor: Julianna Dunn
Project manager: Claire Parkyns, QBS Learning
Copyeditor: Tania Pattison
Proofreader: Janette Schubert
Maps: Sarah Woods, Gordon MacGilp and Ewan Ross
Cover design: Kevin Robbins and Gordon MacGilp
Cover image: Ritu Manoj Jthani/Shutterstock
Production: Rachel Weaver

MIX
Paper from
responsible sources
FSC™ C007454

This book is produced from independently certified FSC™ paper to ensure responsible forest management.

For more information visit: www.harpercollins.co.uk/green

Contents

1 Personal development

1 Read 1.1 and 1.2 in the Student's Book. Match the words below to their definitions. All the words relate to who we are.

a) identity

i) what is morally right and wrong

b) personal qualities

ii) a feature or quality that others can use to define an individual

c) characteristic

iii) the only one of its kind

d) heredity

iv) everything that makes you who you are

e) ethics

v) what you inherit through your genes

f) individuality

vi) the combination of personal characteristics that make up your character

g) unique

vii) characteristics or traits that make you who you are

h) personality

viii) something that makes you different from others

2 Write the words in the box below in the correct place in the diagram.

curious	easily upset	empathetic	noisy
patient	trusting	talkative	caring
messy	shy	calm	bossy

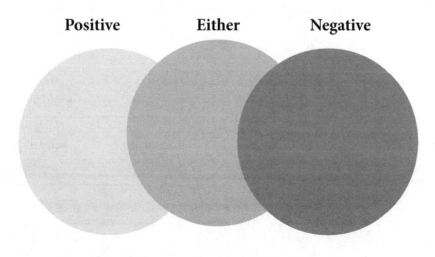

Positive   Either   Negative

3 Choose four words for each circle that describe you. Try to think of words that have not been used in the Student's Book.

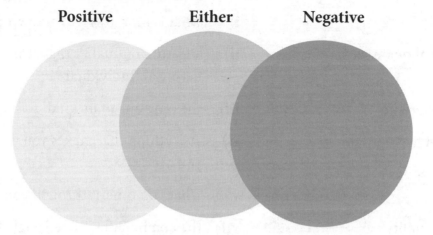

Positive   Either   Negative

4 Circle the word in each group below that does not belong with the rest. These words relate either to heredity or to the environment. Say why the word you circled does not belong in each group. Then write a sentence for each of the words that you circled.

a) skin colour   attitude   genes   blood type

_____

b) peers   school   society   eye colour

_____

c) culture   optimistic   friendly   pessimistic

_____

d) siblings   neighbours   cells   family love

_____

e) loss of a parent   your voice   divorce   family conflict

_____

f) colour of hair   freckles   look like   language

_____

5 Find the words listed below in the word search puzzle. These words relate to aspects of ourselves. The words can be horizontal, diagonal or vertical and may be spelled back-to-front.

D	Y	H	V	V	I	Y	T	L	M	I	H	A	E	K
W	F	Y	N	W	J	C	A	M	G	T	V	Z	C	T
N	V	H	I	M	D	C	D	Q	G	B	U	S	N	F
X	I	C	N	O	I	S	S	A	P	M	O	C	A	H
E	G	C	E	S	N	A	I	F	X	T	R	P	R	A
A	L	U	Y	A	T	L	A	Q	U	I	P	C	E	S
M	E	H	R	X	E	O	A	R	M	R	G	T	L	P
S	P	P	S	J	L	Z	O	N	E	U	N	W	O	E
G	A	S	V	Z	L	S	S	C	O	S	O	R	T	C
L	H	X	Q	D	E	O	I	U	X	I	P	G	L	T
X	E	T	H	I	C	A	L	D	M	K	T	E	Z	V
Q	J	F	G	I	T	K	E	Q	Q	J	F	O	C	X
T	N	N	A	I	U	W	O	H	Y	R	E	O	M	T
W	Z	L	O	E	A	C	A	O	V	G	K	Y	A	E
U	X	N	P	A	L	Z	O	A	Y	E	P	I	W	F

social	physical	aspect	compassion
intellectual	respect	emotional	tolerance
appreciation	ethical		

6 Now write the words in alphabetical order.

a) _____   f) _____

b) _____   g) _____

c) _____   h) _____

d) _____   i) _____

e) _____   j) _____

7 Unscramble the family types and then match them with the correct definition below.

a) g n b i s i l   s h u e o d o h l   _____

b) s t i n g i v i   h s i p r e l n o i t a   _____

c) d e x d t e e n   l y m a f i   _____

d) d o l b o   s i t e   _____

e) g l i n e s   t r a p e n   m y f i l a   _____

f) p h i n k s i   _____

g) r e t e d u t n o c s i t   l y i m a f   _____

h) c r u n l a e   a l i m f y   _____

i) _____ one parent living with his or her children

ii) _____ a larger family, with additional family members besides the nuclear family and with several generations

iii) _____ a family in which the parents are absent, so the older brothers and sisters take care of younger siblings

iv) _____ the most basic form of human relationship, based on blood ties or unions such as marriage or adoption

v) _____ a mother, father and their children living together in one household

vi) _____ relationship where the mother and child live together and the father visits from time to time

vii) _____ a family in which one or more parents have children from previous relationships

viii) _____ a connection based on common ancestry, such as having one or more shared parents or grandparents

8 **Answer these questions about functions of the family.**

a) Name the five functions of the family.

i) _____   iv) _____

ii) _____   v) _____

iii) _____

b) Write your own definition of each of the five functions.

i) _____

ii) _____

iii) _____

iv) _____

v) _____

c) Which of the five functions of the family refers to having children?

_____

d) Beliefs and traditions, morals and values all form part of the cultural function of families. (Circle one.)

                    True   False

e) The economic function of a family means that some members have to work or provide an income for the basic needs of:

i) _____   iii) _____

ii) _____   iv) _____

f) Children learn from their family how to interact and communicate with others, and how to form relationships. This is called _____.

g) Part of a family's function is to provide for the _____ needs of its members through love, attention and support.

9 **Complete the family words using the clues given.**

a) household tasks, such as cooking, cleaning, etc.

d _ _ _ _ t _ _   _ o _ _

b) your brother or sister

_ i _ _ _ n _

c) your father's father and mother's mother

g _ _ _ _ p _ _ _ _ _ _

d) where you come from

_ _ _ g _ _ _

e) genealogical diagram that shows a family

_ a _ _ _ _   t _ _ _

f) behaviours that groups of people do and have done for a long time

_ u _ _ _ _ s

g) the person who earns the main income for a family

_ _ e _ _ _ i _ _ _ r

h) you should always show this to your parents and elders

r _ _ _ _ _ t

10 **Now write a sentence using each of the words from Exercise 9.**

a) _____

b) _____

c) _____

d) _____

e) _____

f) _____

g) _____

h) _____

11 Read 1.10–1.14 in the Student's Book and complete the crossword. All the words are related to conflict, conflict resolution and self-esteem.

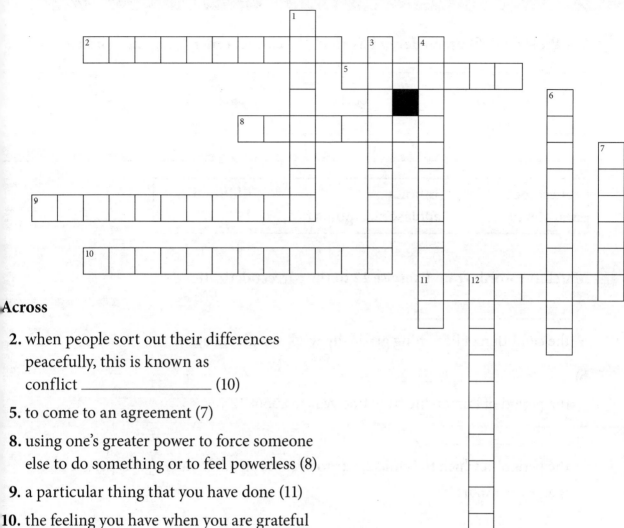

Across

2. when people sort out their differences peacefully, this is known as conflict _____ (10)

5. to come to an agreement (7)

8. using one's greater power to force someone else to do something or to feel powerless (8)

9. a particular thing that you have done (11)

10. the feeling you have when you are grateful to someone (12)

11. a plan of action (8)

Down

1. a serious struggle between two sides with differing needs, views or interests (8)

3. a process in which a third person assists two conflicting people or groups to talk to each other and reach resolution (9)

4. a principle of pardoning another person, or letting go of a grudge or hard feelings you may hold against them for past actions (11)

6. how satisfied you feel about yourself; how much you like and value yourself (4, 6)

7. to feel under-appreciated and not loved is to feel un _____ (6)

12. process whereby two or more individuals or groups can find a peaceful solution to their disagreements (10)

12 Put the stages of human development in the correct order using the words in the box.

☐ →	☐ →	☐ →	☐ →	☐

senescence	infancy	childhood
adulthood	adolescence/puberty	

13 Match the words from Exercise 12 to the correct definition.

a) _____

the condition of becoming gradually weaker with old age

b) _____

the period of human life from one year to about 12 years

c) _____

the period in which the child starts to become an adult; during this period there
is a growth spurt

d) _____

the first year of human life, from being a newborn baby to a one-year-old child

e) _____

the period from about 18 years onwards, when a person is fully grown

14 Read 1.16, 1.17 and 1.18 in the Student's Book. Use the words in the box below to
complete the blank in each sentence.

emotional changes	sexual attraction	risk	hormone
testosterone	physical changes	independence	oestrogen

a) My daughter values her _____ and enjoys driving herself to school.

b) Most adolescents go through many _____ during their early teenage years.

c) _____ among teenagers is common, but entering a sexual relationship carries many risks.

d) _____ is a chemical substance produced in the body that causes men to develop the physical features that are typical of males.

e) Many adolescents find themselves taking a _____ that can involve danger.

f) My teenage sister seems to be going through many _____ that are affecting how she feels and thinks.

g) _____ is a hormone that helps to develop female sex characteristics.

h) A _____ is a chemical substance that controls growth and sexual development.

15 Read 1.16 and 1.17 in the Student's Book. Write a journal entry of about 250 words about what it is like growing up in Form 1. Below are some words to help you.

Journal Entry

| physical changes | emotional changes | puberty | adolescence |
| change | hormones | independence | embarrassed |

1 Complete the crossword. All the words are related to 2.1 in the Student's Book.

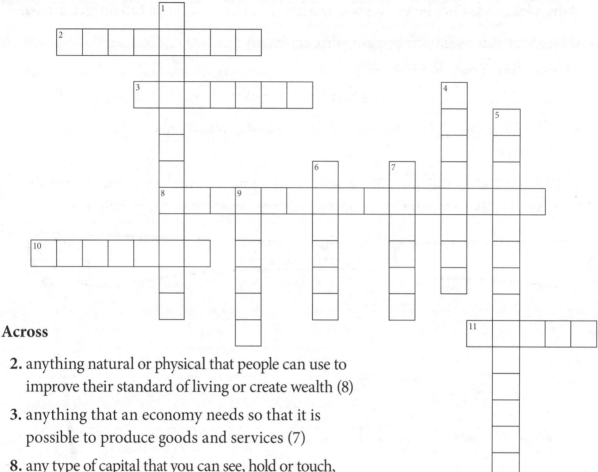

Across

2. anything natural or physical that people can use to improve their standard of living or create wealth (8)

3. anything that an economy needs so that it is possible to produce goods and services (7)

8. any type of capital that you can see, hold or touch, such as cash, machinery, natural resources (8, 7)

10. something one is able to do, for example, the ability to read or tie one's shoelaces (7)

11. material objects that people can see or touch and which they can buy in order to satisfy needs and wants (5)

Down

1. the types of capital that are made up of people and their skills, abilities, talent and knowledge, such as management, training, employees (5, 7)

4. activities that people provide in an economy, for example, teaching, plumbing (8)

5. employees, workers or personnel and their various skills and abilities (5, 9)

6. a special natural ability that makes a person particularly good at something (6)

7. the work that people do to provide goods and services (6)

9. specific learned or developed abilities, such as driving a car (6)

2 Read 2.2 in the Student's Book. Choose words from the box to complete the paragraphs below.

highly skilled	quality	skills development	unskilled	population pyramid
quantity	semi-skilled	composition	skilled	

Factors influencing human resources

There are many factors that affect the growth of human resources. The first is the
(1) _____ of people capable of working in a population. A small country has a
smaller work force available, whereas a larger country has more human resources.

A second factor is **(2)** _____ – the measure of excellence of a country's human
resources. This is related to a country's standard of education. In this context, education
refers to schools, colleges, universities, training centres and programmes that improve
the skills of adults. Some of this **(3)** _____ is provided by the country,
economy or companies who offer education and training for the work force so that they can
improve their current skills and learn new ones.

In addition, population **(4)** _____ shows the make-up or characteristics of the
people in a population. This includes gender, age, ethnicity, occupation and religion as well as
other factors. The age and sex distribution can be seen in a **(5)** _____, where
the population numbers, given in thousands, is numbered in both directions along the bottom
axis, showing male and female numbers. The side axis refers to the different age groups.

A country's human resources are further divided according to how skilled they are.
For example, **(6)** _____ workers do not have any particular skills and are often
employed as cleaners or labourers. **(7)** _____ workers, however, have been trained
to use machinery or tools, and might drive a fork-lift or a tractor. On the other hand, a
(8) _____ worker has some training in a specific field and can work without
supervision, whereas someone who is **(9)** _____ has specialised training and
skills and can often supervise other workers.

3 Refer to the graph and answer the following questions. You may want to use a ruler to
help you.

a) How many females aged 40 will there be
   in 2050? _____

b) How many males aged 60 will there be
   in 2050? _____

c) Which age range will have the highest
   number of females in 2050? _____

d) Which age range will have the highest
   number of males in 2050? _____

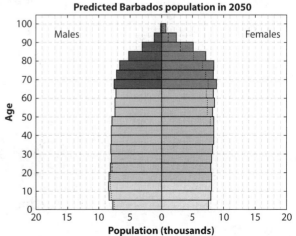

Predicted Barbados population in 2050

15

4 Unscramble each word and then match them with the correct definition below. All the words relate to human resources and economic development.

a) ahnum crusereo plevedtomen

  _____

b) dastrand fo gniliv

  _____

c) yaqutil fo file

  _____

d) no het boj inragnit

  _____

e) pshomtrine

  _____

f) nuitiot stanciasse

  _____

g) eeeylopm

  _____

h) necusicoss tarignin

  _____

i) _____ someone who is paid to work for someone

ii) _____ the degree of wealth and material comfort that a person or community enjoys

iii) _____ training that a worker gets while they are working

iv) _____ training an employee to prepare them for promotion

v) _____ having a colleague appointed as someone to advise and oversee your progress

vi) _____ educating and training the workforce

vii) _____ the level of health, comfort and happiness that an individual or group enjoys

viii) _____ a process whereby an employer pays for the employee's further training

5 Write the words in the box in the correct places in the diagram. All the words relate to activities that form part of economic development.

> incentive programmes   mining   highways   schools
>
> attracting investment   communication   hospitals   tourism   skills
>
> development programmes   ICT   setting up development projects
>
> parks   business development programmes   roads

Creating jobs
_____
_____
_____

Investing in growth industries
_____
_____
_____

Investing in education
_____
_____
_____

Providing infrastructure
_____
_____
_____

Building and maintaining amenities
_____
_____
_____

6 Write 150 words on how tourism benefits your country. Use an extra sheet of paper if necessary.

_____

_____

_____

_____

_____

7 **Read 2.5 in the Student's Book. Answer the following questions.**

a) In what year did the Independence Constitution of Saint Kitts and Nevis take place?

i) 1976   **iii)** 1983

ii) 1985   **iv)** 1973

b) Who is known as the 'Father of Modern Nevis'?

c) Circle the correct answers about Dr Simeon Daniel.

i) He was one of the founding members of the Nevis Reformation Party.   True   False

ii) He was the second Premier of Nevis.   True   False

iii) He founded the Bank of Nevis in 1985.   True   False

iv) He was the Premier of Nevis between 1982 and 1993.   True   False

d) Who was the the first (and only) Premier of Saint Lucia?

_____

e) What year did Sir John Compton become Premier of Saint Lucia?

i) 1986   **ii)** 1967   **iii)** 2003   **iv)** 1987

f) Sir John Compton played a role in helping to establish:

i) CARICOM   **iii)** the government of Saint Vincent

ii) the Organisation of Eastern Caribbean States (OECS)   **iv)** the government of Jamaica

g) In what year was Sir John Compton appointed Prime Minister in Saint Lucia?

_____

h) Which of the following is Sir John Compton **NOT** remembered for?

i) being a statesman   **iii)** modernising Saint Lucia

ii) fighting for people's rights   **iv)** introducing pineapples to Saint Lucia

8 Read 2.6 in the Student's Book. Complete the words about health and health concerns using the clues given.

a) How long people are expected to live, on average, in a country.

_ i _ _   _ x _ _ _ t _ _ c _

b) People live longer and enjoy a better standard of living.

q _ _ _ _ _ _   _ f   l _ _ _

c) The number of children that die before the age of one.

_ _ _ a _ _   _ _ _ t _ _ _ _ _   _ _ t _

d) Any issue that affects people's health in a particular place.

h _ _ _ _ _   c _ _ c _ _ _ _

e) Data measures that indicate how healthy or unhealthy a population is.

_ _ _ _ t _   _ _ d _ _ _ t _ _ s

f) Care available to pregnant mothers and mothers who have recently given birth.

_ _ _ e _ _ _ _   _ _ _ e

9 Do some research and write two paragraphs totalling approximately 250 words on the topic of infant mortality rates, beginning your paragraphs with 'The rates of infant mortality decrease in countries where ...'. Use an extra sheet of paper if necessary.

_____

_____

_____

_____

_____

_____

_____

_____

10 Read 2.8–2.10 in the Student's Book. Draw lines to match the results to the causes of illnesses. Several causes can go with more than one result.

Result	Causes
diabetes	alcohol use
	traffic accidents
	smoking
substance abuse	physical inactivity
	stress
	obesity
	poisoning
cancer	violence
	unhealthy diet
	suicide
accidents and injuries	mental illness
	exposure to the sun
	poor diet

11 Write a letter explaining in about 200 words the problems the government of your country may face with an ageing population. Think about medical care, standard of living, wellbeing and so on.

12 Read 2.10 carefully in the Student's Book and answer each of the questions.

a) Name the three groups that healthy lifestyles benefit.

_____

_____

b) How do exercise and healthy eating affect an individual?

_____

_____

c) Name three ways we can improve our health.

_____

_____

d) How does a healthy workforce benefit the country?

_____

_____

e) What is a healthy individual able to do?

_____

_____

f) Name one voluntary charity organisation in the Caribbean that educates people about lifestyle choices.

_____

_____

g) What three main reasons do people give for not having a healthier lifestyle?

_____

_____

h) What do some companies provide for their workforce?

_____

_____

3   History

1   **Carefully read 3.1 in the Student's Book. Match the correct year to the event.**

| | British rule was finally established with the Treaty of Versailles in Saint Kitts. |

| | Christopher Columbus spotted Saint Kitts and Nevis. |

| | Dame Eugenia Charles was elected Prime Minister of Dominica. |

| | Slavery was abolished throughout the British Empire. |

| | The sugar industry closed down in Saint Kitts. |

| | Saint Lucia gained independence. |

| | The first English settlers arrived on Saint Kitts. |

| | The first French settlers arrived on Saint Kitts. |

| | The Great Hurricane became the deadliest hurricane on record. |

| 1493   1538   1623   1780   1783   1834   1979   1980   2005 |

2   **Read 3.2 in the Student's Book. Then read the two texts below and answer the questions that follow.**

Primary and Secondary Sources

Text One

The film *Swiss Family Robinson* was shot on the island of Tobago in 1959. It cost $4.5 million and took 22 weeks to make. Despite being perfect for filming, the one big problem facing the production crew was that there were no animals on the island. Therefore tropical birds, ostriches, zebras, baby elephants, monkeys, snakes, tigers and an assortment of other animals were flown in with their trainers.

Text Two

2nd April

We are shooting 'Swiss Family Robinson' on the island of Tobago. We have spent nearly 22 weeks here and spent a total of $4.5 million. After deciding to film here, we had to deal with the problem of bringing in large numbers of animals – there were none on the island. Every day around four, all 14 animal trainers come to me and say, "Mr Annakin, what attitude do you want from my animal tomorrow?" So we discuss the next day's filming and they work all night to train their animals.

a) Which text is a primary source?

_____

_____

b) What helped you decide which sort of text it is?

_____

_____

c) Which text is a secondary source?

_____

_____

d) What helped you decide which sort of text it is?

_____

_____

e) Which text was written by someone who was there?

_____

_____

f) Which text was written by a cinema historian?

_____

_____

g) What sources would you need to read to find out about the personal experiences of filming _Swiss Family Robinson_?

_____

_____

h) What sources would you need to read to find out about the history of Tobago?

_____

_____

3 Read 3.1-3.3 in the Student's Book and complete the crossword.

Across

2. your grandparents and great-grandparents (9, 7)

4. a period of 10 years (6)

5. form of relationship based on blood ties (7)

9. a period of 100 years (7)

10. the belief in the existence of God (8)

11. a list of sources that you consult when doing research (12)

Down

1. a document or object created at the time (7, 6)

3. a document created after an event took place (9, 6)

6. where you were born (5, 2, 5)

7. a period of 25–30 years (10)

8. things that people do that are traditional or usual (7)

4 Complete the table about you and your grandparents. When you have finished, discuss your ideas with a friend. Did you have similar ideas? Would you like to have been born when your grandparents were?

AREAS TO COMPARE	YOU	YOUR GRANDPARENTS
Food, such as fast food, home-cooked food		
Subjects studied at school – are they the same?		
School uniforms – are they similar or different?		
Local facilities, such as libraries		
Forms of entertainment, such as coffee bars, cinemas		
Sports – did they do the same type of sports activities?		
Free-time activities – are they the same?		
Personal possessions, for example, clothes, jewellery		
Any other ideas		

5 Write a journal entry about your day at school 50 years ago using the words below.

Journal Entry

curriculum	extra curricular activities	
sports	head teacher	community
library	traditions	uniform

6 Read 3.6 in the Student's Book. Then read the questions and circle True or False.

a) All schools now have science laboratories and improved sports facilities.

     True   False

b) New technology is now used in classrooms.

     True   False

c) Education in the Caribbean has always been compulsory.

     True   False

d) Good academic achievements will help you get a place at university.

     True   False

e) More girls went to school in the past than boys.

     True   False

f) Teachers provide students with good learning experiences.

     True   False

g) A legacy of academic or sporting success can often inspire current students.

     True   False

h) Playing a sport well might assist in becoming a professional sportsperson in the future.

     True   False

7 Write a paragraph about someone who used to attend your school and has inspired you in some way. Say what they are doing now and why you admire them.

_____

_____

_____

_____

_____

_____

_____

 Read 3.8 in the Student's Book about the life of Dame Georgiana Ellen Robinson and then answer the following questions.

a) In what field of social work, in Antigua and Barbuda, did Dame Georgiana Ellen Robinson work?

_____

_____

b) For what purpose did Dame Nellie open her school in 1898?

_____

_____

c) What problem did she identify for children whose parents were not married?

_____

_____

d) What three things did Dame Nellie identify as preventing children from going to Anglican schools?

_____

_____

e) What other accomplishments did Dame Nellie achieve?

_____

_____

f) Name the various awards that Dame Georgiana Ellen Robinson was presented with.

_____

_____

9 Read 3.9 in the Student's Book about the life of Sir George F. L. Charles and answer the following questions.

a) What contribution did Sir George Charles make to Saint Lucia?

_____

_____

b) What political party did Sir George help to form and what did he achieve in 1951?

_____

_____

c) Explain why Sir George Charles was awarded a knighthood.

_____

_____

10 Read 3.10 in the Student's Book about the life of Dame Ruth Nita Barrow and answer the following questions.

a) What contribution did Dame Ruth Nita Barrow make to Barbados?

_____

b) Dame Nita was passionate about providing quality healthcare to the poor. Why was this?

_____

c) Why do you think Dame Ruth Nita Barrow was appointed a dame?

_____

11 Read 3.11 in the Student's Book about the life of Sir Eric Gairy and answer the following questions.

a) What was the policy 'land for the landless'?

_____

b) Why do you think Sir Eric Gairy was known as the 'Father of the Nation'?

_____

c) Why do you think Sir Eric Gairy was knighted?

_____

12 Carefully read 3.13 in the Student's Book. Match the words in the box to the correct heading in each circle.

democratically elected	celebrate	aeroplanes	ships
pastures	vote	cars	festivals
represent	urban areas	pesticides	fertilisers
traditional customs	plantations	governor	buses

Government

_____

_____

_____

_____

Community life

_____

_____

_____

_____

Transport and travel

_____

_____

_____

_____

Farming

_____

_____

_____

_____

1 Read 4.1 and 4.2 in the Student's Book and complete the crossword.

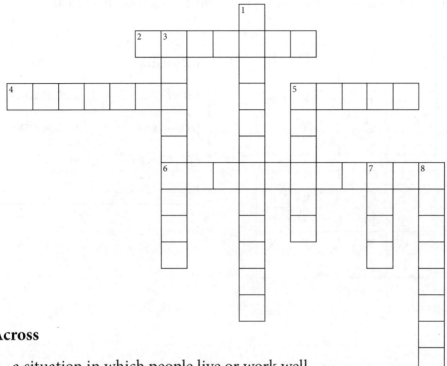

Across

2. a situation in which people live or work well with each other (7)

4. show others you care about their feelings and their wellbeing (7)

5. statements saying what someone can or cannot do in a particular system, game or situation (5)

6. official rules that control the way things are done (11)

Down

1. the results or effects of something (12)

3. someone who has the power to make decisions or tell other people what to do (9)

5. something you receive for good behaviour (6)

7. to do what a law, rule or regulation says you must do (4)

8. a penalty for violation of the law (8)

2 Find the words to reveal the hidden message. The words can be horizontal, diagonal or vertical. All the words relate to rules and regulations in 4.2 and 4.3 of the Student's Book.

B	P	U	N	I	S	H	E	D	R
S	E	R	U	L	E	S	A	E	T
A	L	H	R	E	M	E	G	S	N
N	E	A	A	N	T	U	T	T	E
C	B	O	H	V	L	E	L	R	M
T	A	P	U	A	I	S	L	I	T
I	L	I	T	V	E	O	T	C	A
O	O	I	G	E	T	H	U	T	E
N	O	E	R	S	W	A	L	R	R
N	P	R	O	D	U	C	E	R	T

punished	regulation
label	behaviour
producer	sanction
treatment	strict
laws	

Hidden message:

_____

_____

3 Read 4.4 in the Student's Book and then match the words to their definitions. Each word is related to the laws we follow.

a) constitution   i) agreement among all the people involved

b) compromise   ii) a way of solving a problem when people accept they cannot have everything they want

c) conflict   iii) change and improve

d) consensus   iv) a set of basic rules or principles of a country

e) consultation   v) discussion between people before they make a decision

f) amend   vi) reject, not to approve

g) veto   vii) angry disagreement between people or groups

4 Complete the table with some of the rules you have to follow at home and the consequences of disobeying them. Then write if you agree or disagree with the rule. Say why you would like to change it.

RULE	CONSEQUENCE OF DISOBEYING	AGREE OR DISAGREE?

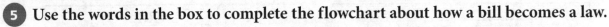

5 Use the words in the box to complete the flowchart about how a bill becomes a law.

signature of Governor-General	debate, amend, vote	introduction of bill
assent stage	bill available for consideration	

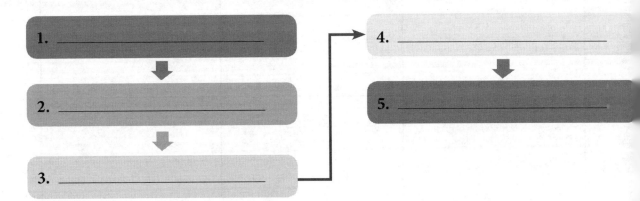

1. _____

2. _____

3. _____

4. _____

5. _____

6 Read 4.4 in the Student's Book. Use the words or expressions in the box to complete each sentence.

assent stage	debate	Governor-General's signature
amend	become law	vote

a) The bill could _____ as soon as next month.

b) There has been a lot of _____ about the proposals by the government.

c) All the bill needs now is the _____ and it will be law.

d) I think the bill is still going through the _____ and hasn't been signed yet before it becomes law.

e) Every citizen aged 18 or over has the right to _____ .

f) The government say they are going to _____ the law to avoid any further misunderstandings.

7 Read 4.5 and 4.6 in the Student's Book and then match the words to form expressions.

a) freedom   i)   responsibility

b) human   ii)   aid agencies

c) civic   iii)   freedom

d) democratic   iv)   parties

e) political   v)   rights

f) fundamental   vi)   and freedoms

g) rights   vii)   of association

h) international   viii) state

8 Read 4.5 and 4.6 in the Student's Book. Use the words in the box to complete the blank in each sentence.

public official	aid agencies	right	UDHR
entitled	declaration	civic responsibilities	citizen

a) Every _____ of your country has the same rights and freedoms.

b) We are all _____ to vote once we are 18 years old.

c) Everyone has the _____ to vote when they are 18 years old.

d) Your _____ are what you have as a citizen of your country.

e) She is a _____ and subject to scrutiny by the public.

f) A _____ is an official document saying that something is true or now law.

g) Several _____ rushed to help people after the natural disaster.

h) The _____ was adopted by the United Nations in 1948.

9 **Read 4.4 to 4.6 in the Student's Book. Answer the questions to complete the activity.**

a) Write down three rights and freedoms that the people of Trinidad and Tobago have.

_____

_____

_____

_____

b) Name three rights people have according to the Universal Declaration of Human Rights.

_____

_____

_____

_____

c) Identify three civic responsibilities of the people in your country.

_____

_____

_____

_____

d) Name two articles in the UDHR.

_____

_____

e) Explain what a 'public consultation' is.

_____

_____

_____

10 Write about the origins of the Universal Declaration of Human Rights (UDHR) and its purpose.

_____

_____

_____

_____

_____

11 Read 4.7 in the Student's Book about Humanitarian Law. Write the words below in the correct boxes.

prisoners of war	types of weapons used	punished	methods of warfare
war crimes	courts of law	the wounded	

The main features of humanitarian law are:

protect

_____

_____

_____

restrict

_____

_____

_____

justice

_____

_____

_____

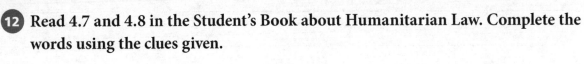

12 Read 4.7 and 4.8 in the Student's Book about Humanitarian Law. Complete the words using the clues given.

a) the types of weapons that are used in war

_ _ t _ _ d _   _ _   _ _ r _ a _ _

b) international laws which aim to limit the effects of war

_ _ _ _ _ i _ _ _ _ _ n l _ _

c) the need and right to honour and respect

d _ g _ _ _ y

d) illegal event during a time of conflict

w _ r   c _ _ m _

e) way of keeping safe or free from injury

_ _ _ t _ _ t _ _ _

f) a fight or battle in which weapons are used

_ _ _ _ d   _ _ _ _ l _ _ _

g) danger to yourself

_ _ r _ _ _ _ _   _ i _ _

h) an act that helps a person in need

_ _ m _ _ _ _ a _ _ _ _   a _ _

i) armed conflict between people

_ _ _

j) fair treatment and punishment when laws are broken

_ _ s _ _ _ e

13 Answer the questions by filling in the gaps about organisations that help with humanitarian acts.

a) The Peace Corps, consisting of _____, go to areas like West Africa.

    i) farmers   **ii)** doctors   **iii)** teachers   **iv)** volunteers

b) The Peace Corps helps with _____, teaching and nursing.
    i) medicine
    ii) vaccinations
    iii) community development
    iv) donations

c) Action Against Hunger helps people who are suffering through drought, floods or war.

                                True   False

d) Doctors Without Borders do not travel to places where there has been a natural disaster.

                                True   False

e) The doctors and nurses of Doctors Without Borders often put their own lives in danger.

                                True   False

f) Habitat for Humanity in the Caribbean works to _____
    i) help homeless people.
    ii) prepare for natural disasters.
    iii) raise money.
    iv) teach people first aid.

14 Imagine that you are a volunteer for the Red Cross Society. Write a letter to a friend telling them how to prepare for a hurricane. Write about 150 words. Continue on a separate sheet of paper if necessary.

_____

_____

_____

_____

1 **Answer the questions and complete the statements based on your reading of 5.1 and 5.2 in the Student's Book.**

a) Name three cultural backgrounds that we have in the Caribbean.

_____

b) Write your own definitions of i) heritage, ii) multicultural and iii) cultural background

_____

_____

_____

c) Identify three celebrations mentioned in the texts.

_____

d) What is CARIFESTA?

_____

e) The two main tribes of the Amerindians were the (i) _____
and the (ii) _____. Group (i) were part of the people known as
_____ and group (ii) were the _____.

f) The Amerindian main crop grown was (i) _____, but they also
cultivated (ii) _____, (iii) _____,
(iv) _____, (v) _____, and (vi) _____.

g) The legacy of the Amerindians lives on today in food:

(i) _____, (ii) _____, (iii) _____

and drink: (iv) _____, (v) _____.

h) Put the arrival of these people to the Caribbean in the correct order.

French	Amerindians	Spanish	Dutch	British

_____

_____

_____

_____

_____

2 Read 5.1 and 5.2 in the Student's Book. Unscramble the following words and then match the words to the definition.

a) r e l t e s t   _____

b) c u r l t u a l   d r u c k g n a b o   _____

c) m i s n o c o i a l l   _____

d) t i l u m - r u l c a u l t   _____

e) r e p i m i m a i l s   _____

f) p r e i m e   _____

g) g r e a t h e i   _____

h) t e l u c r u   _____

   i)   consisting of many cultures

   ii)   the beliefs and traditions that a group of people share

   iii)   the cultural traditions that we have inherited from past generations

   iv)   a group of countries ruled by a queen or king

   v)   someone who comes to live in a country

   vi)   the way a group of people act and think that makes them special

   vii)   a policy of expanding a country into other lands through the use of force if necessary

   viii) the policy of gaining control over land in an other country and exploiting the wealth of the other country

3 Write a letter to a friend telling them about your cultural background. Think about where your ancestors were born. What languages do you speak? What food do you eat, and so on? Write 200–250 words. Continue on an extra sheet of paper if necessary.

_____

_____

_____

_____

_____

_____

_____

_____

4 **Match the events with the correct date in the timeline.**

1627	1492 (December)	1783	1635	1629	1492	1797

a) _____ Christopher Columbus arrived in the Caribbean.

b) _____ First Spanish settlement in Caribbean. Fort La Navidad built on Hispaniola.

c) _____ French settled Martinique and Guadeloupe and used them as a base from which to capture other Caribbean islands including Saint Lucia and Grenada.

d) _____ Saint Christopher (Saint Kitts) was divided between the French and English.

e) _____ Spanish attacked Saint Kitts and Nevis.

f) _____ British forces captured Trinidad.

g) _____ Saint Vincent became an English colony.

5 **Read 5.4 in the Student's Book. Circle the letter of the word or phrase that best completes each sentence.**

a) Many immigrants came to the Caribbean over the centuries, bringing with them their own languages, religions and cultural practices, resulting in a _____ society.
   i)   multilingual
   ii) multireligious
   iii) multicultural
   iv) multiethnic

b) People who speak more than one _____ are multilingual, making the Caribbean a multilingual region.
   i)   religion
   ii) language
   iii) cultural background
   iv) ethnic

c) Many people in the Caribbean speak other languages because of where their
_____ came from.
  i) slaves
  ii) labourers
  iii) immigrants
  iv) ancestors

d) The Caribbean is a multireligious region, so there are many different religious
_____ in the country.
  i) practices
  ii) freedoms
  iii) Baha'ists
  iv) skills

e) The people of the Caribbean are allowed the freedom to practise their own religious
_____.
  i) beliefs
  ii) industries
  iii) plans
  iv) indenture

f) An _____ group is a group of people who have a common cultural
background.
  i) ancestors
  ii) economy
  iii) indentured
  iv) ethnic

g) The Caribbean is a _____ region, because there are so many people from
different cultural backgrounds.
  i) cultural
  ii) multiethnic
  iii) legacy
  iv) business

h) Each ethnic group has different _____ traditions.
  i) economic
  ii) legacy
  iii) cultural
  iv) business

6 Find the words linked with national identity, patriotism and heritage listed below in the word search puzzle. The words can be horizontal, diagonal, vertical, backwards or forwards.

festival	patriotism	cuisine	national identity
historical site	arts and crafts	respect	folklore
ethnicities	religion		

N	A	T	I	O	N	A	L	I	D	E	N	T	I	T	Y
H	K	P	E	P	T	O	E	J	T	R	Y	O	A	L	O
H	I	Q	Z	Y	Q	R	I	H	L	C	E	K	R	A	Z
L	V	S	U	C	O	N	N	G	I	H	V	V	T	V	H
W	A	X	T	L	E	I	X	V	I	U	B	C	S	I	Y
N	S	X	K	O	C	N	E	Y	T	L	V	A	A	T	D
D	U	L	U	I	R	E	K	F	I	L	E	E	N	S	N
Q	O	C	T	C	U	I	S	I	N	E	R	R	D	E	U
F	V	I	V	U	W	R	C	R	M	R	W	B	C	F	I
L	E	X	B	F	I	Y	E	A	A	F	U	D	R	W	O
S	D	D	X	O	G	Y	N	S	L	Z	O	S	A	L	Q
M	S	I	T	O	I	R	T	A	P	S	J	C	F	E	H
J	O	M	N	K	F	J	J	L	S	E	I	I	T	P	X
J	N	R	C	V	N	W	A	N	G	P	C	T	S	L	T
A	V	D	Y	C	B	H	Y	B	M	J	W	T	E	Y	C
E	A	G	J	Z	Y	K	C	F	E	K	N	A	Q	O	P

7 Re-read 5.5 in the Student's Book about our diverse cultural heritage. Write below where the different items originally came from.

a) pelau _____

b) the lion and ribbon dances _____

c) the sari _____

d) Anansi _____

e) kuchipudi _____

f) calypso _____

g) bamboo shoots _____

h) Papa Bois stories _____

i) soca _____

j) rumba _____

k) tea _____

l) Orisha dance movements _____

m) Hosay festival _____

n) roti _____

o) curried mango _____

8 **Write a letter to a friend telling him or her about the last festival you celebrated. Tell them the name of it, where it originally comes from and what happens at the festival.**

_____

_____

_____

_____

_____

_____

_____

_____

_____

_____

_____

_____

_____

_____

_____

_____

_____

_____

9 Match the words from 5.7 and 5.8 in the Student's Book to their definitions.

a) co-existence	**i)** maintain in its original state
b) conservation	**ii)** the system of owning people to work for you
c) diverse	**iii)** without conflict
d) commemoration	**iv)** protecting, restoring and preserving
e) preservation	**v)** angry or violent behaviour by people who are protesting about something
f) peaceful	**vi)** very different from each other
g) unrest	**vii)** a celebration in which we remember and show respect for someone or something
h) slavery	**viii)** living peacefully with others

10 Re-read 5.7 in the Student's Book. Complete each sentence with one word in each blank.

helps	generations	understand	traditions	connects
past	belonging	support	conserve	

Our culture:

a) gives us a sense of _____ to a country.

b) inspires us to carry on _____.

c) _____ us to other people.

d) helps us to _____ the past.

e) connects us to the _____.

f) gives us _____ when we have to face difficult situations.

g) _____ us to understand who we are.

Key phrase: If we do not _____ our heritage, future _____ will not understand what it means to be from the Caribbean.

11 Complete the table below about three festivals.

FESTIVAL	WHAT IT COMMEMORATES	WHEN IT TAKES PLACE	ANY OTHER INFORMATION
Diwali			
Emancipation Day			
Eid al-Fitr			

12 Imagine that you went to one of the festivals above. Write a journal entry saying what you did there, what you wore, what you ate, who you were with and if you enjoyed yourself. Write 200 words.

Journal Entry

13 **Complete the crossword. All the words are used in the Student's Book, 5.7–5.9.**

Across

1. features that belong to the culture of a society that were created in the past and have historical importance for that society (8)

2. process of maintaining something in its original state (12)

4. state of living peacefully with others (11)

5. protecting, restoring and preserving (12)

6. to eat little or no food for a period of time, often for religious reasons (4)

8. before any changes have been made (8)

9. the system of owning people to work for you without payment (7)

Down

1. a structure that is important because it is old and interesting or impressive (8, 8)

2. without conflict (8)

3. very different from each other (7)

7. angry or violent behaviour by people who are protesting against something (6)

1 **Read 6.2 in the Student's Book. Complete the statements below.**

a) Christians believe in the Bible, which is in two parts: the _____ and the _____.

b) Christians believe that God shows himself in three ways: the _____, the _____ and the _____.

c) Jesus was _____ by the Romans, but his followers believe he was _____ three days later.

d) Christians also believe that Jesus will return to Earth in a _____.

e) Common practices among Christians include:

  i) using _____ as their main holy book.

  ii) using _____ as their main place of worship.

  iii) using _____ as their main symbol.

  iv) following Jesus' principal teaching of '_____'.

f) Which Christian denomination believes in:

  i) the teachings of John Wesley, and works to help the poor and serve the community? _____

  ii) the Bible as the only source of authority on Christian faith and morals?   _____

  iii) a version of Christianity that began in the 1500s with a teacher called John Calvin?_____

  iv) the Bible and tradition as the sources of authority?   _____

  v) their followers being filled by the Holy Spirit, causing an experience called speaking in tongues?   _____

  vi) the importance of being 'born again' and accepting the Bible?   _____

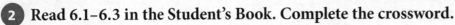

2 Read 6.1–6.3 in the Student's Book. Complete the crossword.

Across

4. a special place for prayers and religious offerings, usually with pictures or statues of religious symbols (6)

5. a ceremony that imparts spiritual grace to those taking part, such as baptism (9)

6. something that you believe to be true about the world (6)

8. brought back to life (11)

Down

1. the process of being reborn in a different body (13)

2. murdered by nailing to a cross (9)

3. affecting everyone or everything (9)

7. a denomination of Christianity that moved away from some of the traditions of the Catholic Church (13)

9. a system of beliefs and practices shared by a group of people (8)

3 **Read 6.3 in the Student's Book about Hinduism and answer the questions.**

a) Where and when did Hinduism begin?

_____

b) Approximately how many people worldwide are Hindus?

_____

c) Where does the word Hindu come from?

_____

d) What is the name of the Hindu universal soul?

_____

e) What is the Hindu belief of returning to Earth many times in different lives?

_____

f) Name the four main goals Hindus work towards.

_____   _____

_____   _____

g) Identify the four paths Hindus follow to moksha.

_____   _____

_____   _____

h) What is a Hindu place of worship called?

A _____ or _____ .

i) What do Hindus have at home where they can worship?

_____

j) Hindus make offerings to a murti, a _____ of a god or goddess.

k) What are the Vedas?

_____

l) What do the Upanishads, part of the Vedas, consider the nature of?

_____

m) When were the Smruti laws written?

_____

n) What are the Puranas, or ancient tales, about?

_____

4   Read 6.4 in the Student's Book about Islam. Imagine you are going to interview a student who is a Muslim. Read the questions you might ask and complete the answers.

a) What does the word 'Islam' mean?

_____

b) Where and when did the religion begin?

_____

c) Upon whose teachings is Islam based?

_____

d) What are the two types of Muslim found in the Caribbean?

_____

e) Why are there two types of Muslim found in the Caribbean?

_____

f) Do you have a holy book?

_____

5   Read 6.5 and 6.6 in the Student's Book about world religions. Use the words in the box to complete the blank in each sentence.

enlightenment	philosophy	covenant	permanent
atheist	compassion		

a) The Sikhs' _____ is to help those in need and live a life of good actions.

b) _____ for Buddhists is a state of full understanding and knowledge of all things.

c) Taoists strive to have _____ for other people, as well as practising moderation and humility.

d) An _____ is someone who does not believe in God.

e) Buddha taught that things change all the time and that nothing is

_____.

f) The Jewish religion teaches that their single God entered into a

_____ with the Jewish people.

6 Imagine you are the friend of a Muslim teenager. Write a brief journal entry about his or her religion using the words below.

Journal Entry

mosque	Qur'an	lunar	fast
muezzin	Hajj	Sunni	Ramadan

7 Read 6.5 and 6.6 carefully in the Student's Book. Match the religions to their beliefs. Use each religion twice.

Judaism   _____   Baha'i faith   _____

Buddhism   _____   Confucianism   _____

Sikhism   _____   Taoism   _____

a) This religion encourages benevolence, duty, manners, wisdom and faithfulness.

b) This religion believes that a person is judged on how they keep the laws and traditions of their faith.

c) This religion believes their followers should lead a life of good actions, especially by serving others.

d) This religion strives for the 'three treasures' – compassion, moderation and humility.

e) This religion believes that an individual should not strive for too much fasting and sacrifice.

f) This religion believes in one God and emphasises the unity of all human beings.

g) This religion believes that, in exchange for God's love and protection, their followers undertake to keep God's laws as per the Old Testament.

h) This religion teaches that life includes much suffering and to end it their followers should live a way of life called the Middle Way.

i) This religion believes that all religions share the same message and purpose – to bring human beings together.

j) This religion focuses on how people should behave in their everyday lives, especially in relationships with others.

k) This religion believes that each reincarnation depends on one's actions in a previous life.

l) This religion shares a close relationship with Confucianism and Buddhism.

8 Read 6.7 and 6.8 in the Student's Book and then complete the table.

RELIGION	PLACE OF WORSHIP	SYMBOL (WRITE THE NUMBER)	WHERE ARE THESE IN YOUR COUNTRY?
Christianity			
Islam			
Hinduism			
Buddhism			
Sikhism			
Judaism			

1.

2.

3.

4.

5.

6.

9 The words below are key vocabulary words from 6.7 to 6.9 in the Student's Book. Match the words to their definitions.

a) crescent

i) a rounded structure over a circular base forming the roof of a building

b) place of worship

ii) a curved shape representing one of the phases of the moon

c) symbol

iii) a symbol made by a long vertical line and a short horizontal line, representing Christianity

d) cross

iv) a picture or sign that represents a particular meaning

e) dome

v) building or place where people gather to pray, meditate or worship

10 Read 6.9 in the Student's Book. Write the words in the box in the correct place on the diagram.

cathedrals	music	the Last Supper
frescoes	spires	the Temptation of Christ
vices	domed ceilings	illuminated writing
evil	the Nativity	paintings

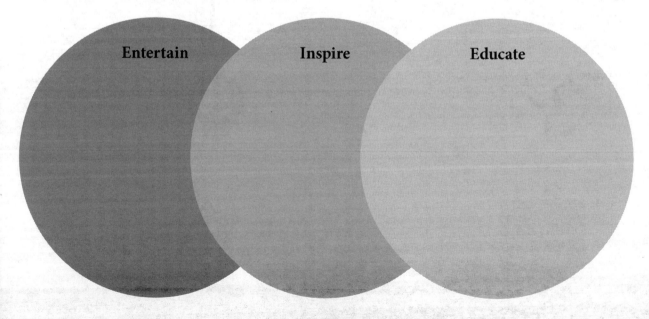

Entertain   Inspire   Educate

11 Unscramble each word and then match them with the correct definition below.

a) t h o m y g o y l   _____

b) n o n t h a p e   _____

c) r a t u i l   _____

d) m a t r o l i m   _____

e) a r m a d   _____

   i) _____ a body or collection of myths or stories belonging to a people and addressing their origin, history, deities, ancestors and heroes

   ii) _____ all the gods of a people considered as a group

   iii) _____ a play for the theatre

   iv) _____ able to live forever

   v) _____ a formal ceremony in which the actions and wording follow a prescribed form and order

12 Write 200 words on how religion affects your life. Think about how big a part it plays in your daily life and say what you like and dislike about it.

_____

_____

_____

_____

_____

_____

_____

_____

_____

_____

_____

_____

_____

_____

1 Look at the map below and label the following countries a–k:

a) Anguilla

b) Antigua and Barbuda

c) Montserrat

d) Dominica

e) Saint Lucia

f) Barbados

g) Saint Vincent and the Grenadines

h) Grenada

i) Grand Cayman

j) Guyana

k) Saint Kitts

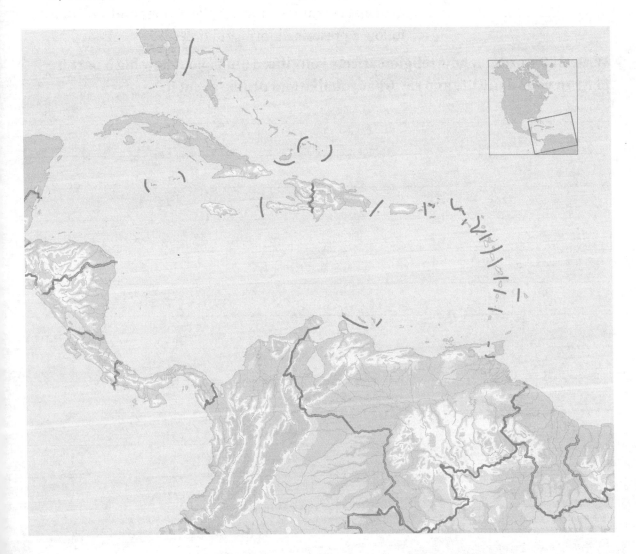

2 Complete the crossword. All the words are from 7.1 to 7.3 of the Student's Book.

Across

6. a country that is controlled and often exploited by another country (6)

9. a country that is dependent on a mother country (10)

11. areas that are not part of the built environment (7, 11)

12. I _____ and value the place I live (10)

Down

1. a large mass of land that forms the main part of a country, but does not include any islands (8, 9)

2. independent countries that used to form part of the British Empire (12)

3. the weather conditions in an area (7)

4. large areas of land that are usually divided into several countries (10)

5. a country that has colonies or dependencies (6, 7)

7. animals that live in the sea (6, 4)

8. the place where the land meets the sea (9)

10. low area often covered with water from the lake, river or sea next to it (7)

3 Can you identify these flags?

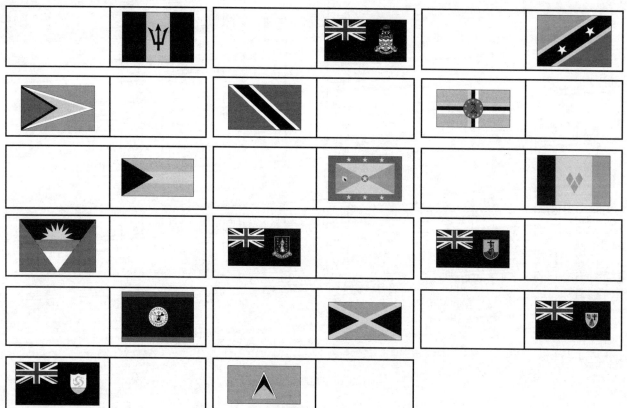

4 Read 7.5 and 7.6 and circle the correct answers.

a) What do the Commonwealth Caribbean countries all have in common?

i) they all have exactly the same physical features

ii) they are all connected by ships

iii) they all border the Atlantic Ocean

iv) they are all located in and around the Caribbean Sea

b) What is not the same in all Caribbean Commonwealth countries?

i) climate

ii) rainfall

iii) coastal areas

iv) natural disasters

c) What is special about the Caribbean Sea?
   i) it covers a small area
   ii) the water is cold
   iii) it is the largest sea in the world
   iv) it is a freshwater sea

d) What do the Caribbean Commonwealth countries only have a few of?
   i) rivers and lakes
   ii) waterfalls
   iii) long rivers
   iv) mountains

e) What natural disaster can affect some of the Caribbean Commonwealth countries?
   i) earthquakes
   ii) heavy rainfall
   iii) dry rivers
   iv) forest fires

f) How many people in the Caribbean region are thought to have roots in India?
   i) 12 million
   ii) over 2.5 million
   iii) more than 40 million
   iv) 40 per cent of the population

5 **Write a letter to an overseas friend explaining why so many tourists visit Trinidad and Tobago. Write 250 words.**

_____

_____

_____

_____

_____

_____

_____

_____

_____

_____

6   **Read 7.7 in the Student's Book and then answer the questions.**

a) What is the Caribbean organisation that promotes regional integration and cooperation among its members?

_____

b) What does the organisation do for the Caribbean community?

_____

c) How many member states does the organisation have? How many can you name?

_____

d) Name the six main agricultural items grown in the Caribbean Commonwealth.

_____

e) Apart from the Caribbean, where else do the Caribbean Commonwealth countries export their agricultural produce?

_____

f) What successful industries can be found in Trinidad and Tobago?

_____

g) Name two manufacturing industries in Jamaica.

_____

h) What is an important service industry in Barbados?

_____

i) Citizens of CARICOM countries can move around and work in any CARICOM country and this promotes links between them. True or False?

_____

j) How do tourists travel from one Caribbean country to another?

_____

7 Match the countries of the Caribbean to their capital cities.

a) Anguilla		**i)**	St John's
b) Antigua and Barbuda		**ii)**	Rouseau
c) Barbados		**iii)**	George Town
d) Cayman Islands		**iv)**	Basseterre and Charlestown
e) Dominica		**v)**	Kingstown
f) Montserrat		**vi)**	The Valley
g) Saint Kitts and Nevis		**vii)**	Castries
h) Saint Lucia		**viii)**	Port of Spain
i) Saint Vincent and the Grenadines		**ix)**	Plymouth
j) Trinidad and Tobago		**x)**	Bridgetown
k) Grenada		**xi)**	Georgetown
l) Guyana		**xii)**	St. George's

8 Read 7.7 and 7.8 in the Student's Book. Match the words or expressions to their definitions.

a) capital city

i) important or big urban area

b) economic factors

ii) things that relate to trade, industry, occupations and wealth

c) industry

iii) the business of making goods in large quantities in a factory

d) town

iv) economic activities related to farming

e) agriculture

v) economic activities such as transport, banking, tourism, communications or utilities

f) main city

vi) the urban area where the government is based

g) services

vii) an urban area that is smaller than a city

h) manufacturing

viii) economic activities where systems supply a public need, such as manufacturing

9 Look at the map and complete the activity.

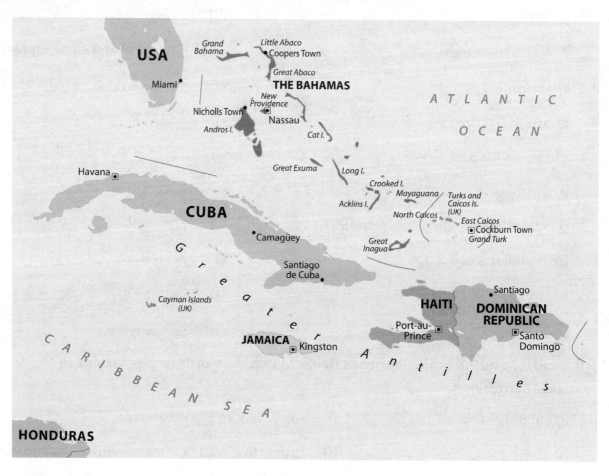

a) Name the capital city of The Bahamas.

_____

b) Which island is the capital of The Bahamas on?

_____

c) In which ocean are The Bahamas situated?

_____

d) Name two countries to the south of The Bahamas.

_____

_____

e) Identify two other large cities or towns of The Bahamas.

_____

10 **Look at the map and complete the activity.**

a) Name the capital city of Trinidad.

_____

b) Name the capital city of Saint Vincent and the Grenadines.

_____

c) In which ocean are all the islands situated?

_____

d) Name two countries to the south of Dominica.

_____

e) Name the island to the east of Saint Vincent and the Grenadines.

_____

f) Which islands are included in the group of islands known as the Windward Islands?

_____

g) Which island is situated between Trinidad and Tobago, Barbados and Saint Vincent and the Grenadines?

_____

h) Which island is situated to the north of Saint Vincent and the Grenadines?

_____

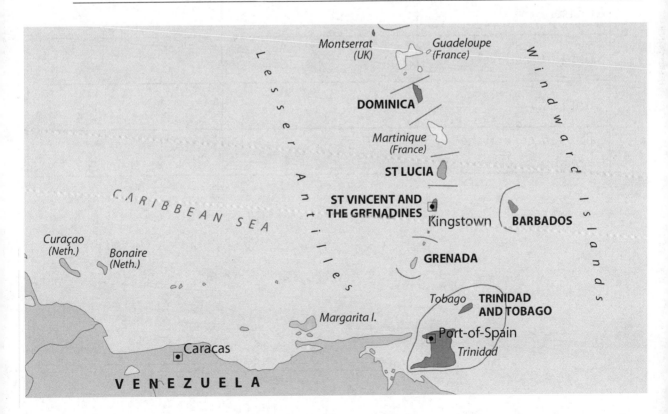

11 Read 7.11 in the Student's Book. For each of the countries write the name of the head of government and their title in the table below.

COUNTRY	NAME	TITLE
Anguilla		
Antigua and Barbuda		
Barbados		
Dominica		
Grand Cayman		
Grenada		
Guyana		
Montserrat		
Saint Kitts and Nevis		
Saint Lucia		
Saint Vincent and the Grenadines		

1 Fill in the gaps in the key to show which natural resources can be found in Guyana.

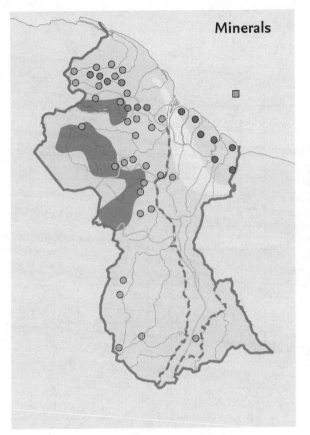

Key

Key

2 Complete the crossword. All the words are from 8.1 to 8.4 in the Student's Book.

Across

2. long length of pipe laid over the ground or underground (8)

4. occurring in large amounts per square unit of area (12)

7. able to be seen or touched (8)

8. the process of cutting or digging stone or land to obtain minerals (9)

10. anything that we use from our environment in order to produce goods or services (9)

11. our physical and human surroundings; the world around us and all that is in it (11)

12. interconnected systems of living organisms and the features of their environment (10)

Down

1. a factory where oil gets converted into other chemicals (8)
3. an area thickly covered with trees and shrubs (6)
5. vessel that carries oil or natural gas (6, 4)
6. places where minerals are found (8)
9. the sets of members of population living at a particular time (11)

3 Circle the word in each group that does not belong with the rest. They are all to do with the environment and are used throughout Unit 8. Say why the words do not belong. Then write a sentence for each of the words that you circled.

a) gravel   acrylic   limestone   sand

_____

_____

b) pesticides   solid waste   fertilisers   herbicides

_____

_____

c) by-products   recycling   organic farming   mulching

_____

_____

d) smog   purify waste   carbon monoxide   dust

_____

_____

e) sulphur oxide   dioxides   chemical blanket   algae

_____

_____

f) high yield   monocrop   loss of biodiversity   soil erosion

_____

_____

4 Imagine you have just spent a day on a farm. Write a journal entry about what you did there. Include the words from the box below. Write 200 words.

Journal Entry

sustainable	irrigation	monocropping
fertiliser	habitats	ingest
maximise	high yield	crop rotation

5 Read 8.9–8.12 in the Student's Book. Put the words in the box under the correct heading in the table.

reduce	produced water	non-renewable
coal	oil spills	carbon footprint
energy-efficient	reuse	cholera
turn off appliances	gaseous emissions	eutrophication
consumer culture	water-wise plants	free range
industrial waste	compost heap	landfills
detergents	ethical consumer	carbon dioxide
sewage	crude oil	rubbish

WATER POLLUTION	IMPACT OF FOSSIL FUELS	CARING FOR THE ENVIRONMENT	RESPONSIBILITY FOR OUR ENVIRONMENT

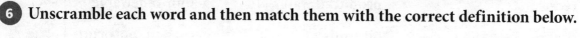

6 Unscramble each word and then match them with the correct definition below.

a) t r e s n n u i t _____

b) w o n n b r e n e l e a _____

c) c r o s e m u n t r u c l u e _____

d) g a s e w e _____

e) c i l a t h e c r u m o n s e i s m _____

f) d a c i n a i r _____

g) t r a w e s i w e _____

i) _____ the belief in buying new products or valuing things that are new

ii) _____ human faeces, urine and wastewater from laundry and washing

iii) _____ making careful choices about what you buy in order to show your ethical values

iv) _____ using water efficiently to save as much as possible

v) _____ organic compounds that help plants and micro-organisms to grow very fast

vi) _____ liquid that contains high levels of acidic compounds that can corrode buildings

vii) _____ something that we cannot grow more of or replenish; it will run out

7 Complete the mind map which outlines some solutions for air pollution. Use the words in the box.

purify waste	release gases	control	dispose properly
more by foot	burning	prevention	fines

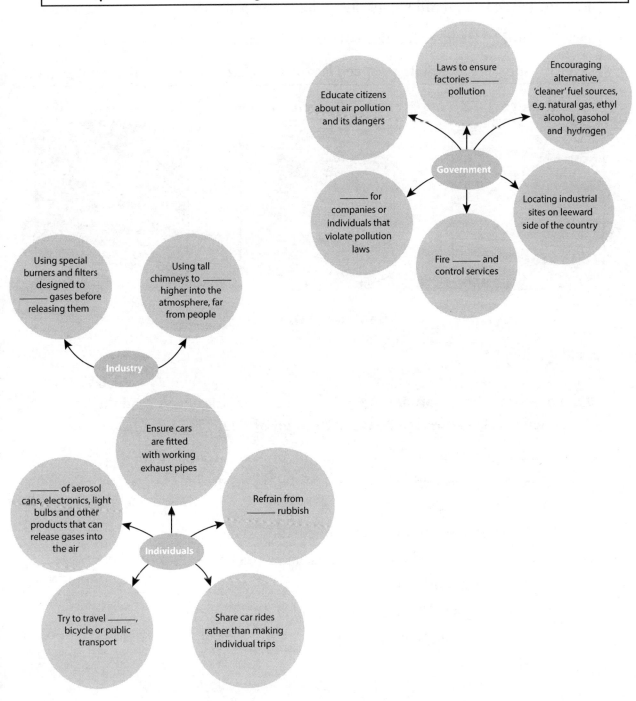

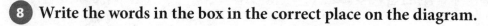
8 Write the words in the box in the correct place on the diagram.

less land needed for landfills	plastic	buy fewer products	glass	aluminium
have less stuff	less need for disposal services	paper	saving of natural resources
reduce disposable materials	spend less on bags, jars, bottles	don't put in bags

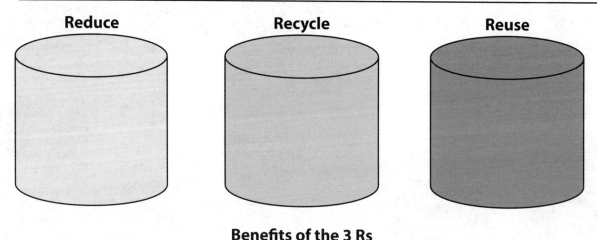

Reduce **Recycle** **Reuse**

Benefits of the 3 Rs

9 Look at 8.16 in the Student's Book about natural disasters. Read the statements below and write D for Drought or F for Flood against each one.

a) buildings and other structures may be damaged or destroyed

b) loss of crops, as well as lower milk and meat production, as cattle may get sick or die

c) not enough food for the human population due to famine

d) waste can be carried into reservoirs, lakes and rivers

e) waterborne diseases may spread

f) soil erosion caused by wind moving over dry land

g) people and animals may drown

h) bush fires

10 Look at 8.16 and 8.17 in the Student's Book about natural disasters. Circle True or False for each of the statements below.

a) Landslides can occur when there is heavy rain or when floodwaters move over the rocks.   True   False

b) Landslides can bury homes, farms, animals and people.   True   False

c) Tsunamis are generally caused by a volcano erupting.   True   False

d) Earthquakes are set off by the movement of the Earth's crust.   True   False

e) A cyclone can measure over 950 kilometres across.   True   False

f) A hurricane is formed when a tropical cyclone moves at more than 33 metres per second.   True   False

g) Tornadoes rarely damage buildings, land or cars.   True   False

h) A tornado is a spinning column of air that forms under thunderclouds.   True   False

i) A dormant volcano may have erupted thousands of years ago, but will not erupt again.   True   False

j) Dominica has a volcano called Kick 'em Jenny.   True   False

11 Read 8.17 in the Student's Book carefully. Match each word to its definition.

a) cyclone   i) has not erupted for a long time, but may be able to erupt again

b) hurricane   ii) a tropical storm with a closed, circulating wind pattern

c) tornado   iii) intense tropical cyclone that moves faster than 33 metres per second

d) dormant   iv) may have erupted thousands of years ago, but is not able to erupt again

e) extinct   v) rotating column of air that forms under a thundercloud

1 **Look at the map of the world below, then answer the questions.**

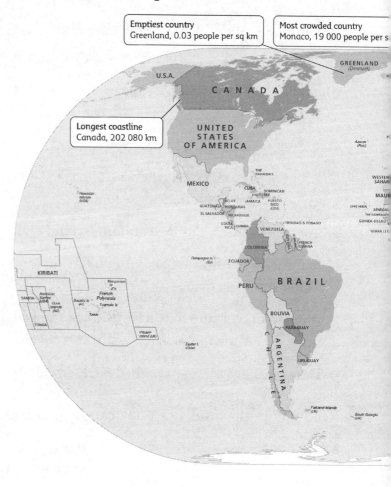

Emptiest country
Greenland, 0.03 people per sq km

Most crowded country
Monaco, 19 000 people per s

Longest coastline
Canada, 202 080 km

a) Mark on the map the names of the continents and oceans and at least one desert, mountain and river.

b) In which country are the most languages spoken?

_____

c) Which country is the smallest in the world?

_____

d) Which country has the least number of people per square kilometre?

_____

e) Which country has the most land boundaries?

_____

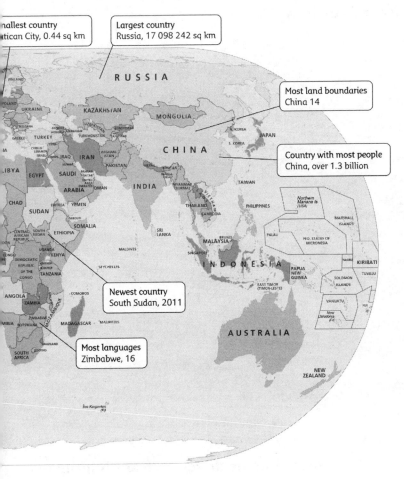

Smallest country
Vatican City, 0.44 sq km

Largest country
Russia, 17 098 242 sq km

Most land boundaries
China 14

Country with most people
China, over 1.3 billion

Newest country
South Sudan, 2011

Most languages
Zimbabwe, 16

f) Name the newest country.

_____

g) Which country has the most people?

_____

h) Identify the largest country in the world.

_____

i) Which country has the longest coastline?

_____

j) Name the country that has the most people per square kilometre.

_____

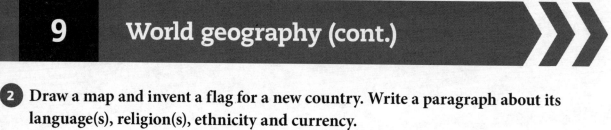

9 World geography (cont.)

2 Draw a map and invent a flag for a new country. Write a paragraph about its language(s), religion(s), ethnicity and currency.

3 Complete the facts about your country. Use the internet to research any information you are not sure about.

Continent	
Population size	
Official languages	
Main religions	
Main ethnic groups	
The name of the national anthem	
The national symbol	
Currency	

4 Look back at the world map on pages 248–249 of the Student's Book. See how many countries you can find for each of the letters A–Z. Add the language that country speaks. Use the internet to research any information you are not sure about. (Clue: some letters may not have countries for them.)

	COUNTRY	LANGUAGE		COUNTRY	LANGUAGE
A			N		
B			O		
C			P		
D			Q		
E			R		
F			S		
G			T		
H			U		
I			V		
J			W		
K			X		
L			Y		
M			Z		

5 Complete the crossword. All the words can be found in 9.1–9.7 in the Student's Book.

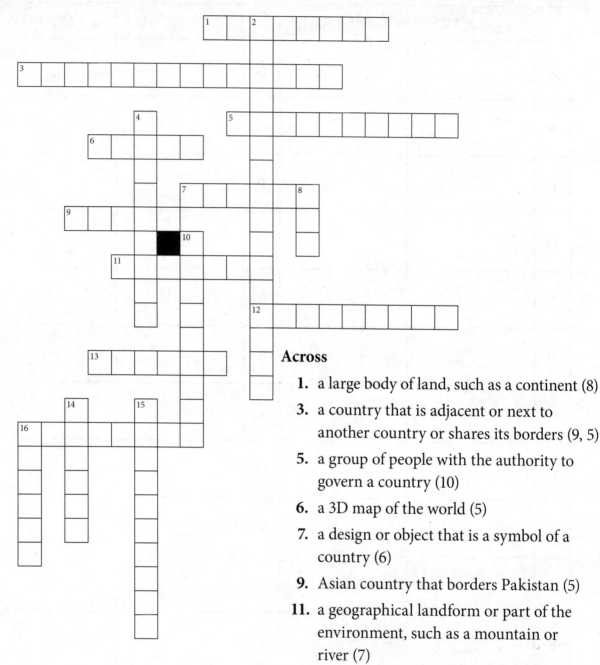

Across

1. a large body of land, such as a continent (8)

3. a country that is adjacent or next to another country or shares its borders (9, 5)

5. a group of people with the authority to govern a country (10)

6. a 3D map of the world (5)

7. a design or object that is a symbol of a country (6)

9. Asian country that borders Pakistan (5)

11. a geographical landform or part of the environment, such as a mountain or river (7)

12. a stream that feeds into a larger river (9)

13. the place where a river starts, usually in a mountain or hill (6)

16. an outline or dividing line; a line that encloses a given area (8)

Down

2. the idea of a nation as a whole; having a shared culture, language or any other shared traits contained in its history (8, 8)

4. one of the large, continuous expanses of land on Earth, such as South America (9)

8. a picture that shows an area of the Earth as seen from above, showing either physical or political features (3)

10. a grouping of people with common national or cultural traditions (9)

14. an examination and record of an area of land, in order to create an accurate plan or description (6)

15. surrounded by other countries (10)

16. edge of a country or a line separating two countries or regions (6)

6 **Read carefully 9.7 in the Student's Book. Circle the correct answers below.**

a) Why do countries have borders?

   i)   to separate them from other countries

   ii) to share mountain ranges

   iii) to establish territorial waters

   iv) to emphasise previous colonial rule

b) What sort of border is a mountain range?

   i)   a man-made border

   ii) a political boundary

   iii) a straight-line border

   iv) a natural boundary

c) What does a straight-line border usually indicate?

   i)   a disputed border

   ii) a neighbour state

   iii) a colonial past

   iv) a landlocked country

d) Why do border disputes arise?

   i)   people have not signed treaties

   ii) some landlocked countries need a coastline

   iii) neighbour states go to war

   iv) countries argue about who should own certain land

e) Lake Chad is the border for how many countries?

   i)   two

   ii) three

   iii) four

   iv) five

7 Look at this political map of the Caribbean. Label the following countries: Anguilla, Antigua and Barbuda, Barbados, Dominica, Grand Cayman, Grenada, Guyana, Montserrat, St. Kitts, St. Lucia, St. Vincent and the Grenadines.

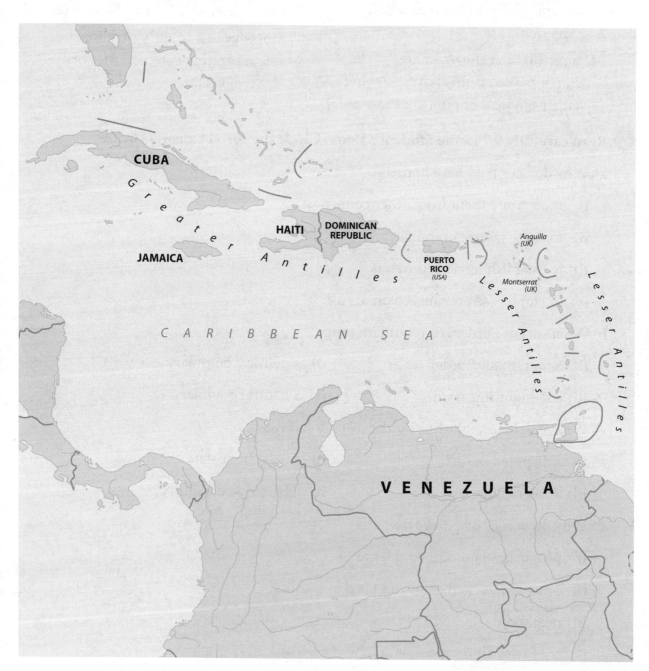

8 Read 9.7–9.9 in the Student's Book. Match the words to their definitions.

a) an area of a town or country   i)   parish

b) a smaller division within a county, usually used   ii)   district
    for voting purposes

c) a territorial division within a country, forming   iii)   demarcation
    the main unit for local administration

d) the act of determining the boundaries or limits of   iv)   ward
    an area

e) a village or town which has its own church   v)   county

9 Write a letter to a pen friend overseas describing the features of your country. Include as much information as you can about the system of government, the capital city, the national anthem, flower, flag and emblem, as well as the physical features such as wetlands, rivers, mountains and coastline. Write 250 words. Use an extra sheet if necessary.

_____

_____

_____

_____

_____

_____

_____

_____

_____

_____

_____

_____

_____

_____

_____

10 Use the maps to answer the questions.

a) What type of border does Paraguay have?

_____

b) What type of border does Chile have?

_____

c) How many countries does Bolivia share its borders with? Name them.

_____

_____

d) What feature is on the Peru/Bolivia border?

_____

e) What is the nearest mainland country to Trinidad and Tobago?

_____

f) Which country shares a border with Guyana and French Guiana?

_____

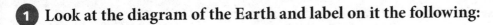

10   The world around us

1 Look at the diagram of the Earth and label on it the following:

The Equator   The Arctic Circle

The Tropic of Cancer   The North Pole

The Tropic of Capricorn   The South Pole

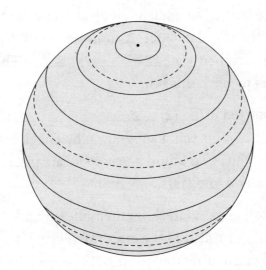

2 Read 10.4 in the Student's Book and complete the paragraph using the words in the box.

Caribbean Sea	Leeward	Antilles	mainland
Windward	reefs	cays	

The Caribbean is made up of many islands, (1) _____, and
(2) _____ _____, as well as some of the (3) _____ countries that
border on the Caribbean Sea. Geographers divide the islands of the
(4) _____ into two clusters: the Greater and Lesser Antilles.

The islands of the Lesser Antilles are divided into:

• (5) _____ Islands in the south

• (6) _____ Islands in the north

• Leeward (7) _____ in the west.

3 **Read 10.2 and use the words in the box to complete the blanks in the text.**

circumference	grid	longitude	geography
astronomer	west	latitude	maps

For thousands of years, people have used the skies to help with navigation.

The Phoenicians were part of an ancient civilisation in the Middle East. They were known for exploring the world by boat. As long ago as 600 BC, the Phoenicians used the sun and stars to work out their **(1)** _____ . The Polynesians also used the movement of the stars to work this out.

The ancient Greeks started using **(2)** _____ lines to show latitude and **(3)** _____ . This was a suggestion by Greek astronomer Hipparchus around 300 BC. Hipparchus also found a way to locate places on Earth by observing the positions of the sun, moon and stars.

Around 225 BC, Eratosthenes, a Greek mathematician and **(4)** _____ , measured the circumference of the Earth (the distance around the Earth) by calculating the distance between Alexandria in northern Egypt and Syene in southern Egypt. Once he worked this out, he was able to work out the **(5)** _____ of the Earth.

This discovery helped the Greeks draw **(6)** _____ as they were able to find their latitude easily using trigonometry and the positions of the sun, moon and stars.

Ancient scholars also made many mistakes in their ideas and writings about **(7)** _____ . The Roman scholar Ptolemy believed that the circumference of the Earth was shorter than it actually is.

As a result, Christopher Columbus made the mistake of believing he could reach Asia by sailing **(8)** _____ from Europe.

4 Complete the crossword of geographical terms.

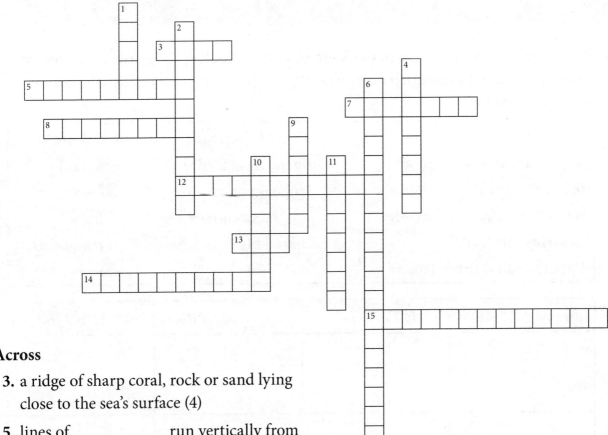

Across

3. a ridge of sharp coral, rock or sand lying close to the sea's surface (4)

5. lines of _____ run vertically from north to south, parallel to the Prime Meridian (9)

7. hemisphere where the Caribbean is situated (7)

8. a continuous stretch of land that makes up the main part of a country, as opposed to offshore islands (8)

12. process of working together (11)

13. a low island composed mainly of coral or sand (3)

14. joined together or working cooperatively as a single unit (10)

15. a process of making the world more connected, with goods, services and people moving and communicating easily and quickly between all parts of the world (13)

Down

1. a small island (5)

2. a country or province controlled by an outside nation (10)

4. lines of _____ run horizontally across the globe from west to east, parallel to the Equator (8)

6. the joining or working together of countries that are geographically near each other in order to make them economically and politically more powerful (8, 11)

9. a piece of land surrounded on all sides by the sea (6)

10. towards the side sheltered by the wind (7)

11. into the wind; on the side facing the wind (8)

5 Read carefully 10.5 and 10.6 in the Student's Book. Look at the words in the box to do with the Caribbean region and integration. Then write them under the correct heading in the table.

free trade	diversifying trade	hurricanes
import and export of goods	liberalising trade	geography
increasing trade	languages	cricket
import and export of services	limited resources	culture
ensuring fair trade	shared history	earthquakes
import and export of labour		storms

SIMILARITIES	HAZARDS	COOPERATION	CARICOM

6 Read 10.7 in the Student's Book. Unscramble each of the clue words. Copy the letters in the numbered cells into the bottom row of cells with the same numbers to find the words linked with maps.

a) HICLASPYPAM

    9 10

b) RODAAMP

  7

c) REEMSOASPRUC

  3

d) LAIOCILPPAMT

         4   2

e) LYBMOS

    11   5

f) WROAR

  8

g) DEELNG

    6

h) LACSE

  1

1 2 3 4 5 6 7 8 9 10 11

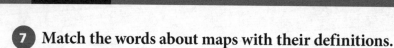
7 **Match the words about maps with their definitions.**

a) bird's-eye-view   i)   a view from directly above the ground

b) observation   ii)   someone who plans and draws maps

c) scale statement   iii)   a scale expressed as a number, ratio or fraction

d) to scale   iv)   the action or process of closely and carefully looking at or monitoring something or someone

e) cartographer   v)   the relationship between distances on a map and distances in real life

f) ratio scale   vi)   a scale showing a line distance and what that distance represents in real life

g) linear scale   vii)   uniformly reduced or enlarged; showing the relationships in proportion to real life

h) map scale   viii)   scale expressed as 1 cm = 1000 km

8 **Look carefully at the maps. Match the correct scale to each map.**

a) Map _____   Scale 1:50 000 000

0   500   1000 1500 2000km

b) Map _____   Scale 1:3 000 000

0   25   50   75   100 125   150km

c) Map _____   Scale 1:11 000 000

0   100 200 300 400   500km

Map 1

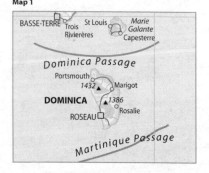

Map 2

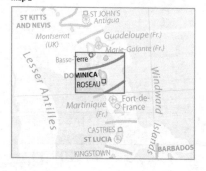

Map 3

9 Look at the map and answer the questions. (Hint: look at 10.9 in the Student's Book about ratio scale.)

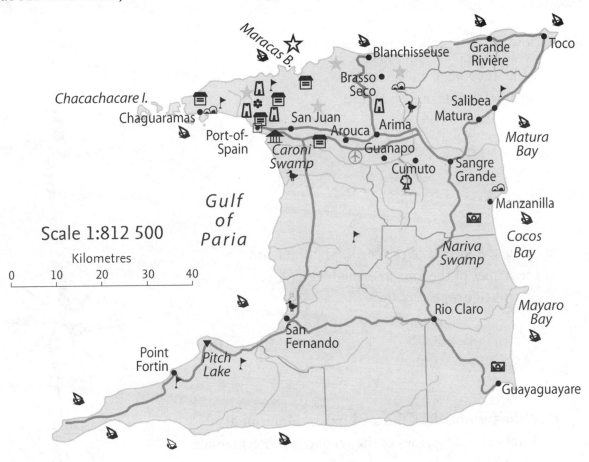

Scale 1:812 500

a) What is the map scale?

_____

_____

b) How far is Pitch Lake from Cocos Bay, as the crow flies?

_____

c) If you drove from Toco to Guayaguayare, how far would you have driven?

_____

d) Imagine you have a boat and are going to sail from Port-of-Spain to Point Fortin. How many kilometres would you have to sail?

_____

e) What is the distance between San Fernando and Rio Claro by road?

_____

10 Follow the instructions to complete the activity.

a) Write the names of the four main
   cardinal points on this figure.

b) Write the initials of the cardinal points and
   the names of the four intermediate points
   on this figure.

c) Write the initials of the cardinal and intermediate
   points and the names of the secondary intermediate
   points on this figure.

11 Read 10.12 in the Student's Book and complete the sentences.

a) Which direction is between south-southeast and south-southwest? _____

b) North-northeast is between _____ and _____.

c) Southeast is between _____ and _____.

d) Northeast is halfway between north and _____.

e) What direction is between southeast and southwest? _____

f) Which cardinal point comes between east-northeast and east-southeast?

   _____

12 Look at the map and answer the questions (Hint: See 10.9 in the Student's Book about using grid lines.)

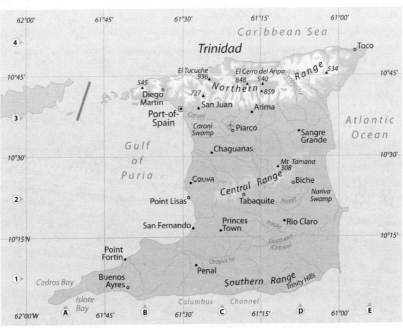

a) What gulf can be found in B3? _____

b) Name the hills found in D1. _____

c) Which swamp can be found in C3? _____

d) Name two towns in C2. _____

e) Which bays are found in A1? _____

13 Using the map above, write down the co-ordinates for the following places.

a) Rio Claro

_____

b) Port-of-Spain

_____

c) The International Airport

_____

d) Toco

_____

e) Mt Tamana

_____